First published by Parragon in 2012

Parragon
Queen Street House
4 Queen Street
Bath BA1 1HE, UK
www.parragon.com

ISBN 978-1-4454-6683-5

Printed in China

GO, GO SAMURAI!

These Samurai Secrets belong to:

_____

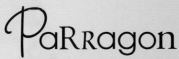

Bath · New York · Singapore · Hong Kong · Cologne · Delhi
Melbourne · Amsterdam · Johannesburg · Auckland · Shenzhen

Contents

Welcome, Ranger Trainee

Centuries ago in Japan, Nighlok monsters invaded our world, but Samurai warriors defeated them with Power Symbols passed down from parent to child. Today, the evil Nighlok have risen once again and plan to flood the Earth. Luckily, a new generation of heroes stand in their way. They are...
The Power Rangers Samurai!

Do you have what it takes to become a Samurai Ranger? Learn the way of the Samurai and help the Power Rangers save the world!

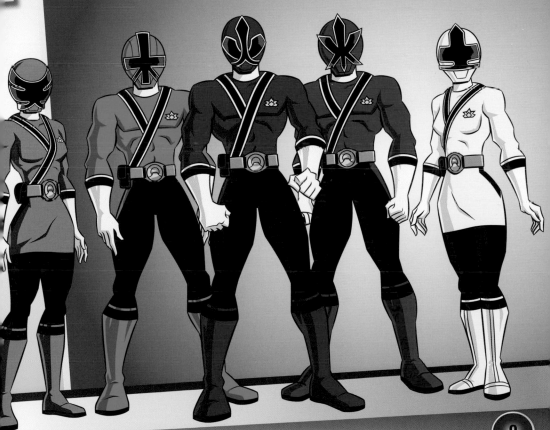

Turn the page to begin your journey as a Power Ranger trainee…

Secret Profile

"Samurai must constantly improve their skills to ready themselves for battle."

Mentor Ji watches over the Power Rangers and teaches them the way of the Samurai. He has been a father figure to Jayden since Jayden was a child. Although he does not fight alongside the Rangers, he has done much

Samurai Challenge!

Mentor says there are three important values you need to be a Samurai:

Patience   Concentration   Discipline

He has set you some tests over the next few pages. Practise hard, trainee!

First, finish these sentences for Mentor...

My favourite teachers are: _____

They have taught me: _____

My top talent is: _____

Mentor Ji

Patience

To be patient you must not get frustrated when things don't work out straight away. Remember, everything takes time and practice!

I showed I was patient when

_____

_____

_____

Now try Mentor's patience challenges...

Code Buster

The Red Ranger is sending a message to the other Rangers.
Can you crack the code to work out what it is?

True Blue

Uh-oh! The Blue Ranger has been cloned! Luckily, the clones all look a little different — can you find the real Ranger? Give 100%, trainee!

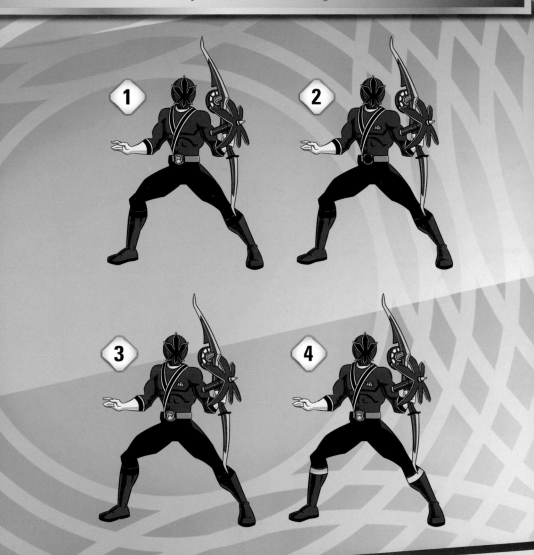

Answer: 3

A Smashin' Time

A creepazoid Nighlok has smashed up the names of some Power Rangers characters! Can you unscramble them?

1 YADJNE

_____

2 IAM

_____

3 VENKI

_____

4 YILEM

_____

5 KEMI

_____

6 PISEK

_____

7 LUBK

_____

Concentration

To concentrate, you must put all of your attention on one thing or action. This can be pretty tough!

The last time I really concentrated was

_____

_____

_____

Now try Mentor's concentration challenges...

Rofer Run

Can you lead the Yellow Ranger through the maze to her ApeZord?
Watch out for Rofer and his giant punching arms!

START

FINISH

Spot the Difference

A good Samurai Ranger must have an eagle eye to be one step ahead of the enemy. Can you find six changes in the second picture?

We're the Samurai Rangers!

Discipline

To be disciplined you must follow the rules and practise your training. Jayden is very disciplined because he's been training his whole life.

I will show I am disciplined by

_____

_____

_____

Now try Mentor's discipline challenges...

Search and Find

Even when things get tough, a Ranger will still keep going!
See if you can find all eight Ranger words in the grid.
Look forwards, backwards, up, down and diagonally.

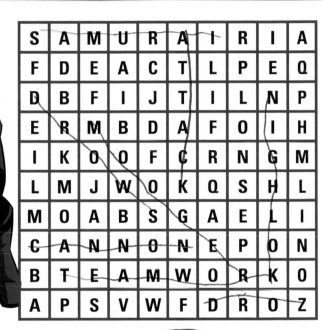

S	A	M	U	R	A	I	R	I	A
F	D	E	A	C	T	L	P	E	Q
D	B	F	I	J	T	I	L	N	P
E	R	M	B	D	A	F	O	I	H
I	K	O	O	F	C	R	N	G	M
L	M	J	W	O	K	Q	S	H	L
M	O	A	B	S	G	A	E	L	I
C	A	N	N	O	N	E	P	O	N
B	T	E	A	M	W	O	R	K	O
A	P	S	V	W	F	D	R	O	Z

SAMURAI   ATTACK
NIGHLOK   SWORD
MOOGER   CANNON
ZORD   TEAMWORK

Which Ranger Are You?

The responsibility of being a Power Ranger is great. Could you do it?
Find out which Ranger you're most like!

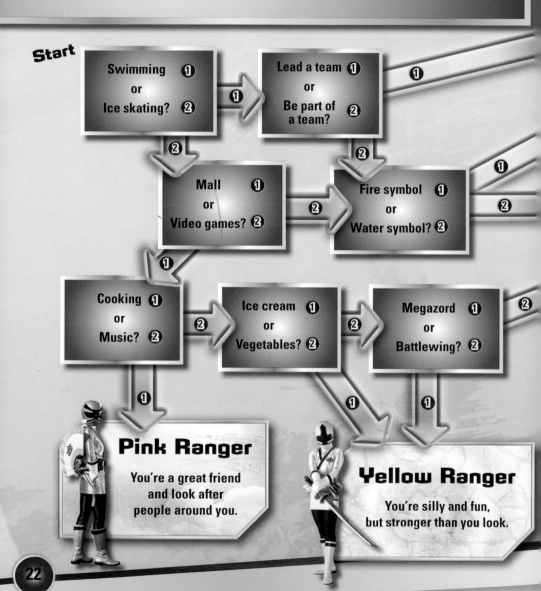

Start

Swimming ①
or
Ice skating? ②

Lead a team ①
or
Be part of
a team? ②

Mall ①
or
Video games? ②

Fire symbol ①
or
Water symbol? ②

Cooking ①
or
Music? ②

Ice cream ①
or
Vegetables? ②

Megazord ①
or
Battlewing? ②

Pink Ranger

You're a great friend
and look after
people around you.

Yellow Ranger

You're silly and fun,
but stronger than you look.

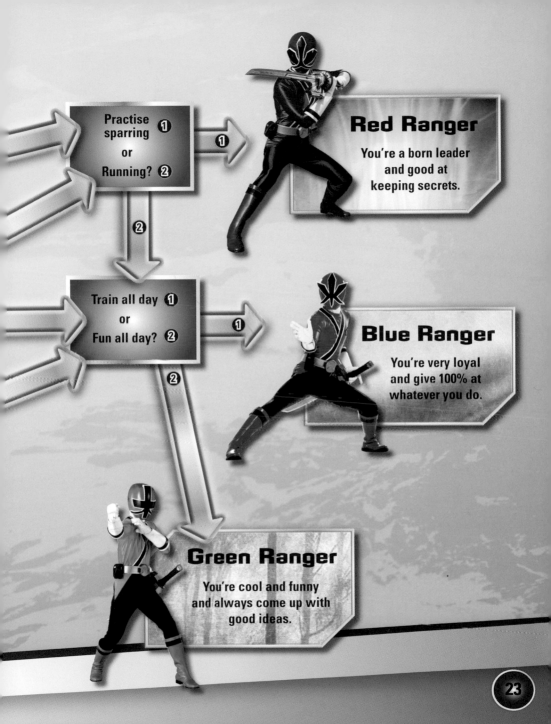

Practise sparring ①
or
Running? ②

① ➡

Red Ranger

You're a born leader and good at keeping secrets.

②

Train all day ①
or
Fun all day? ②

① ➡

Blue Ranger

You're very loyal and give 100% at whatever you do.

②

Green Ranger

You're cool and funny and always come up with good ideas.

23

My Power Ranger Profile

CONGRATULATIONS!

Mentor Ji is very pleased with your training so far. It's time to create your own Power Ranger identity!

My name is _____

My Power Ranger colour is _____

My catchphrase is _____

My weapon is _____

My best Ranger friend is _____

Describe your Ranger personality:

_____

_____

_____

_____

My cool Kanji Symbol is (draw it here)

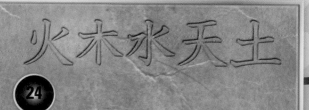

火木水天土

My Samurai outfit looks like this – awesome!
Draw yourself as a Samurai Ranger here.

Secret
Profile

Like his Zord, the lion, Jayden is a strong leader. He doesn't say too much, but when he speaks, he means what he says. Jayden has been raised and trained since he was a child by Mentor Ji. He also has a secret that he must keep from all the other Rangers.

Name: Jayden
Element: Fire
Zord: Lion
Special Weapon: Fire Smasher
Signature Move: Fire Smasher!

"I need to be the best and keep getting better!"

Samurai Code

As the leader of the Power Rangers, Jayden sets an example for the others by living by the Samurai code.

Sign your Ranger name below each statement on the opposite page if you believe in them, too!

Confidence

Every Power Ranger succeeds because they believe in themselves and their friends! Confidence helps them stay strong.

Standing up for what's right

The Power Rangers are always ready to challenge villains and look out for each other.

Health and fitness

Keeping fit and training means the Power Rangers can stay one step ahead of the Nighloks. It is important to exercise and eat well.

Teamwork

Five heads are better than one! By working together, the Power Rangers solve important problems.

Friendship

They may be a team of super heroes out to save the world, but the Power Rangers are friends first! They always help each other out.

Top Secret!

Jayden keeps a mysterious secret from the other Power Rangers. Do you have any secrets? Share them here!

Secret 1
_____
_____
_____
_____

Secret 2
_____
_____
_____
_____

Secret 3
_____
_____
_____
_____

Could you keep Jayden's secrets?

Answer the questions and follow the arrows to see what kind of a secret-keeper you are!

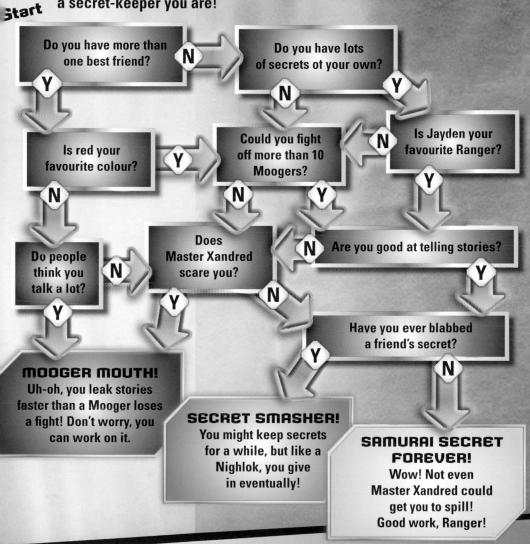

Start

Do you have more than one best friend?

N → Do you have lots of secrets of your own?

Y

Is red your favourite colour?

Y → Could you fight off more than 10 Moogers?

N ← Is Jayden your favourite Ranger?

N

N

Y

Do people think you talk a lot?

N → Does Master Xandred scare you?

N ← Are you good at telling stories?

Y

Y

Y

Y

Have you ever blabbed a friend's secret?

Y

N

MOOGER MOUTH!
Uh-oh, you leak stories faster than a Mooger loses a fight! Don't worry, you can work on it.

SECRET SMASHER!
You might keep secrets for a while, but like a Nighlok, you give in eventually!

SAMURAI SECRET FOREVER!
Wow! Not even Master Xandred could get you to spill! Good work, Ranger!

Secret
Profile

Mia is like a big sister to the Power Rangers. She thinks she's a great cook and the rest of the Rangers try to act like she's right, but they secretly think her food is terrible! One thing they all agree on is that Mia is an important part of their Nighlok-fighting family.

Name: Mia
Element: Sky
Zord: Turtle
Special Weapon: Sky Fan
Signature Move: Airway!

"Sky Fan! Hey, join my *fan* club. No autographs, please!"

Who Said That?

Can you help Mia guess who said what?

1 My team – the whole world – is depending on me!

_____

2 Fear is the enemy. If you believe in yourself you can win any battle.

_____

3 Hydro Bow. Now it's my turn to bring it!

_____

4 I got some new moves to go with my Samurai groove!

_____

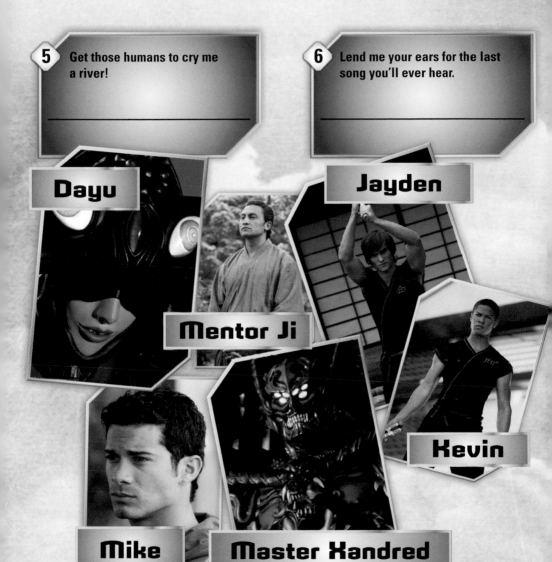

Dayu

Jayden

Mentor Ji

Kevin

Mike

Master Xandred

My Own Zord

Now you have your Ranger profile, you're going to need your own Zord, too! Jayden has a lion and Mia has a turtle – what will yours be?

Pick your favourite animal from this list or add your own.

Eagle	Spider
Mastodon	Panther
Snake	Crocodile
Elephant	Jellyfish
Wolf	Rhinoceros

My Zord is a _____

Which words best describe your Zord? Circle as many as you like.

Loyal	Tough
Brave	Graceful
Magical	Friendly
Fast	Clever

Draw your Zord here. Don't forget to match the colours to your own Ranger suit!

Secret Profile

Mike isn't a troublemaker, but he is a bit of a rebel! He loves video games and hanging out with his friends. He's a talented Ranger with a wild and goofy sense of humour, but this won't stop him from giving his all in every battle!

Name: Mike
Element: Forest
Zord: Bear
Special Weapon: Forest Spear
Signature Move: Forest Vortex

"Let's heat this up for this creepazoid!"

The Green Ranger

Match Zords

Bear FoldingZord, Mega Mode Power! Can you match Mike, the Green Ranger, and the other Power Rangers to their animal Zords? Draw lines to pair them up.

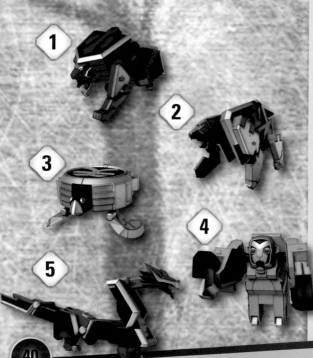

T__ Gr___
Machine!

The Green Ranger comes out with some brilliant put-downs for the Moogers and Nighloks! Can you think of some more? Try a mega rhyme, like his!

"Moogers to the left of me, Moogers to the right, but when I get done with them, they all say goodnight!"

"Oh man, the Moogers! It's a whole school of fish faces!"

_____

_____

_____

_____

Samuraizer Games

Mentor's Mirror

If you can read an enemy's moves then you can outsmart them!

Players should stand facing a friend. Decide who is going to lead – the other person tries to copy the leader exactly. Watch the move first, and then try it together!

Nighlok Invasion

A Nighlok is taking over the minds of humans! The Power Rangers must seek them out and save the civilians!

To start the game, players must choose one person to be the Power Ranger. This person then leaves the room. While the Ranger is gone, a secret Nighlok is chosen, and the rest of the group play humans. When the Ranger returns, the Nighlok should go around the room 'brainwashing' the humans by making funny movements that they have to copy. The trick is for the Ranger to spot the secret Nighlok by closely watching everyone!

Rangers Ready!

Get together with some friends to watch a Power Rangers episode.

Every time one of these things happens, you have to perform the action:

Mentor speaks	→ You say "Yes, Mentor."
You hear "Go, Go Samurai!"	→ Punch your hand in the air as if you're holding a sword!
Someone mentions the Sanzu River	→ Take a gulp of your juice.
Every time you see a Nighlok	→ Shout "Samurai Strike!"
When you first see a Megazord	→ Shout "We are united!"

Secret
Profile

Kevin is a disciplined master swordsman and a professional swimmer. His father trained him from a young age in the ways of the Samurai. He often makes the other Rangers laugh, but when the time comes to get a job done, you want this warrior on your team!

Name: Kevin
Element: Water
Zord: Dragon
Special Weapon: Hydro Bow
Signature Move: Dragon Splash

"Now it's my turn to bring it!"

What's Your Superhobby?

Start

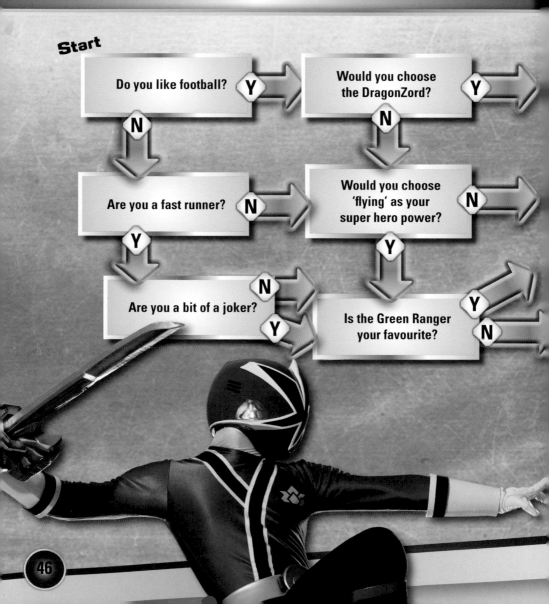

Do you like football? **Y**

Would you choose the DragonZord? **Y**

N

N

Are you a fast runner? **N**

Would you choose 'flying' as your super hero power? **N**

Y

Y

Are you a bit of a joker? **N**

Y

Is the Green Ranger your favourite? **Y**

N

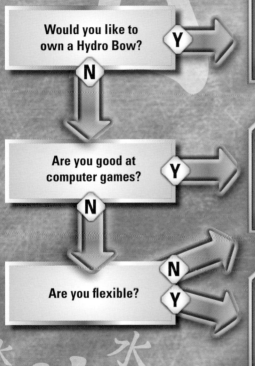

SWORDPLAY STAR

You would be the master of the Rangers' most important weapon – the Spin Sword. Without mastering the sword, you can't progress to the more powerful weapons.

Would you like to own a Hydro Bow? **Y**

N

MEGAZORD DRIVER

The Power Rangers make steering the Megazords look easy, but it's a talent in itself! Use your Mega Blade to drive the Rangers to victory!

Are you good at computer games? **Y**

N

ACROBAT

You've seen the Power Rangers' mega moves – you would be flipping and kicking as well as the Red Ranger in no time!

Are you flexible? **N** **Y**

Ranger Training Exercises

Follow Kevin's lead and prepare for Mooger attacks with these Samurai-smart exercises!

Ranger Jack

- Put your hands on your waist and put your feet shoulder-width apart.
- Jump high and bring your knees up and together and land with your feet together.
- Then jump your feet out to where you started!
- Do five Ranger Jacks. Then rest and do five more.

Crab Crawl

- Sit down on the floor.
- Put your feet out in front of you with your hands behind you.
- Raise up your body on your hands and feet, and crawl around like a crab!
- Can you do it for three minutes?

Samurai Stretch

- Stand with your feet shoulder-width apart.
- Bend your knees, turn to your right, and stretch your left hand out in front of you as far as it will go. At the same time, stretch your right hand behind you.
- Repeat on the other side.
- Do it five times on each side.

Cobra Pose

- Sit on your knees with your hands on your waist.
- Put your hands out in front of you on the floor.
- Now dip your head down towards the floor and push up with your hands while you arch your back like a cobra!
- Now do it in reverse to end up back on your knees!

Secret Profile

Emily is a sweet, innocent country girl who was never supposed to be a Power Ranger. Her sister was meant to be in the team, but she became ill and Emily had to take her place. Everyone loves her silly, fun attitude, and she trains hard to make her sister proud.

Name: Emily
Element: Earth
Zord: Ape
Special Weapon: Earth Slicer
Signature Move: Seismic Swing

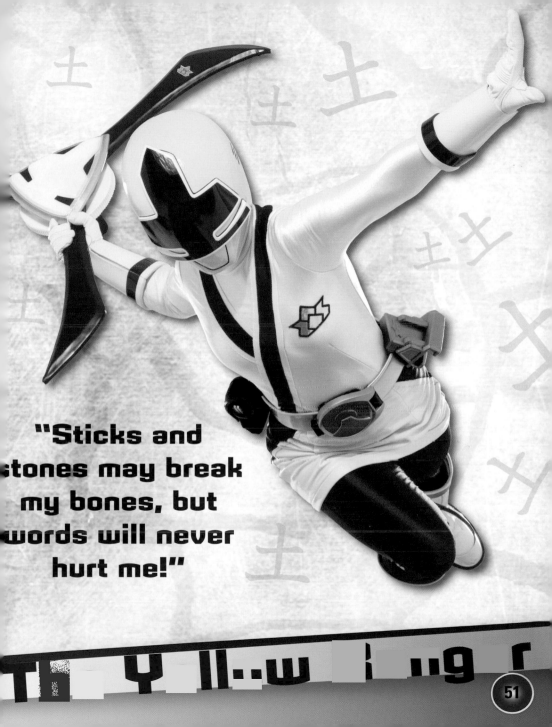

"Sticks and stones may break my bones, but words will never hurt me!"

The Yellow Ranger

Spot the Difference

Concentrate, trainee! Can you find six differences between these pictures of Emily and the other Rangers?

Colour in the Yellow Ranger's symbol for each difference you find.

Gap Sensor... Nighlok Attack!

Power Food Plan

Before you begin training, always be sure to eat right every day, just like Emily. A balanced diet is very important. Check out the Power Rangers' top energy-packed foods!

Fruit

Helps provide vitamins and keeps teeth and gums strong!

Top Tip
Snack on an apple or orange.

Vegetables

Can help to keep eyes and skin healthy!

Top Tip
Vegetables are not the bad guys – give them a chance!

Meat and Beans

Can help build muscle and bones, gives you energy and helps you fight germs!

Top Tip

If you've got more energy, you'll be ready to be a force for good!

Milk

Can help build even stronger bones!

Top Tip

A glass a day keeps the Moogers away!

Grains

Keep your cells healthy and give you energy!

Top Tip

Rangers love porridge and brown rice.

Secret Profile

Antonio is a fun and playful member of the team. He did not have any formal Samurai training and mastered his fighting skills on his own. He is a computer whizz who uses electronic power symbols and even learned how to program his Zords!

Name: Antonio
Element: Light
Zords: OctoZord and ClawZord
Special Weapon: Barracuda Blade
Signature Move: Barracuda Bite

My Samurai Team

Now that you're beginning to master the way of the Samurai, you'll see how important it is to have friends and backup.

Who would be a part of your team? Pick four friends or family members, and then stick photos of their faces, as well as your face, on the picture!

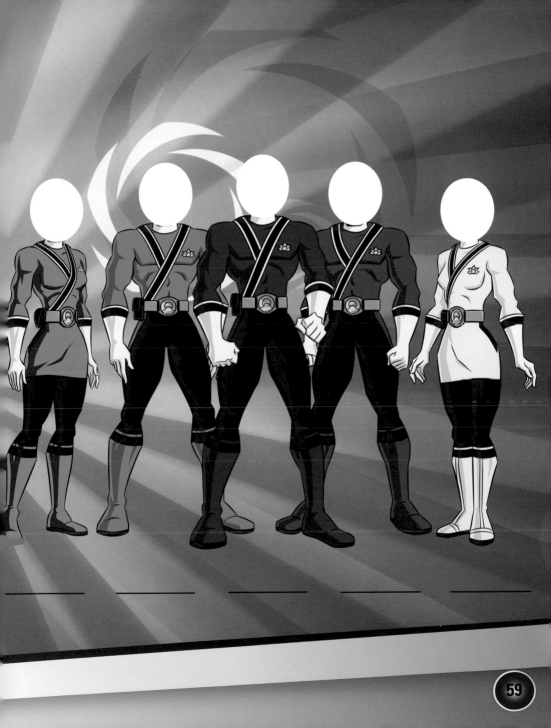

Go, Go Samurai
Adventure

Now that you have your Power Ranger team together, what will your first adventure be? Use these questions to kick-start your ideas!

1) What are you and your Ranger team doing at the start of the story?

A Queuing for the rollercoaster at Rainbow's End.
B Training outside the Shiba House.
C Eating Mia's latest recipe in the kitchen.

2) Which Nighlok comes through a gap into our world?

A Rofer, with long punching arms.
B Doubletone, who tricks people into giving up their dreams.
C Negatron, who can turn emotional pain into physical pain.

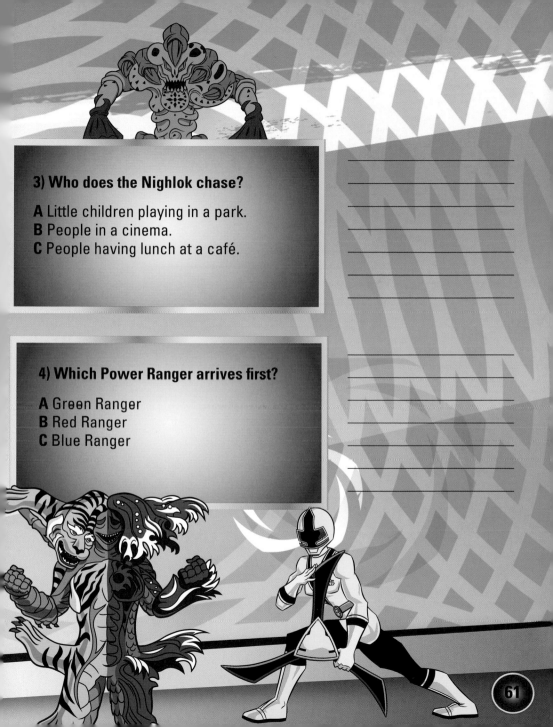

3) Who does the Nighlok chase?

A Little children playing in a park.
B People in a cinema.
C People having lunch at a café.

4) Which Power Ranger arrives first?

A Green Ranger
B Red Ranger
C Blue Ranger

61

5) What special move defeats the Nighlok?

A Dragon Splash
B Airway
C Fire Smasher

6) Who wins?

A The Nighlok
B The Megazord
C Neither – Deker steps in

Draw a picture of your adventure here!

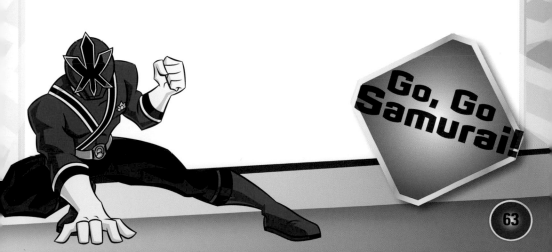

Go, Go
Samurai!

Welcome to the Netherworld

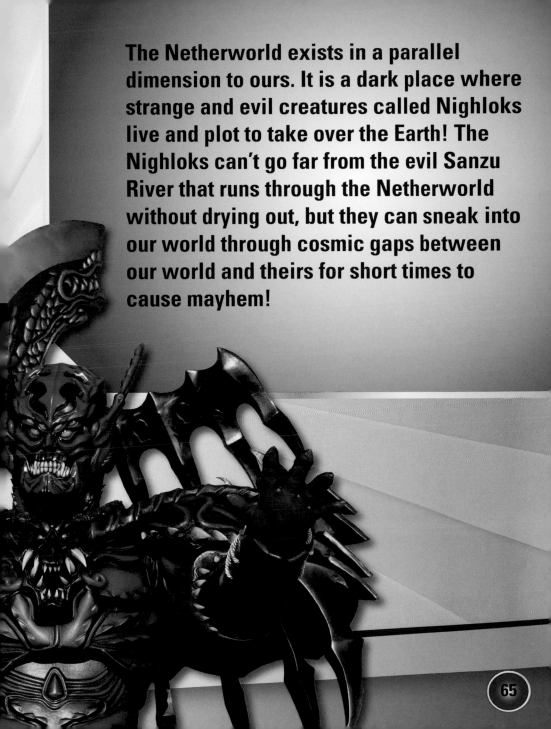

The Netherworld exists in a parallel dimension to ours. It is a dark place where strange and evil creatures called Nighloks live and plot to take over the Earth! The Nighloks can't go far from the evil Sanzu River that runs through the Netherworld without drying out, but they can sneak into our world through cosmic gaps between our world and theirs for short times to cause mayhem!

Watch out, Rangers!

It's Master Xandred and his evil friends! In case you've forgotten what scary looks like, check them out...

Master Xandred

Master Xandred is the leader of the evil Nighlok monsters who live in the Netherworld. He recently reawakened after being shattered into a million pieces years ago by Jayden's father, the previous Red Ranger. He is not yet strong enough to travel to our world, but is determined to escape his Netherworld prison. He plans to flood the evil Sanzu River into our world with the tears of those 'cry-baby humans'.

"Get those humans to cry me a river!"

Octoroo

Master Xandred's advisor is a short, Octopus-like creature (some even call him 'noodle face'!). He advises Master Xandred about the secrets of the Netherworld and the secrets of the Rangers contained in the ancient archives, and suggests the best ways to challenge and defeat the heroes.

"Ooo, ah, ooo! He got a call from Octoroo!"

Deker

Even though he is half Nighlok, Deker has no interest in hurting humans. Instead, he's filled with the desire to fight the ultimate duel and won't find peace until that happens. After witnessing the Red Ranger in battle, he knows he has finally found a worthy opponent. Determined to save him for himself, Deker will at times step in and protect the Red Ranger from other Nighlok attacks!

"Finally – a worthy warrior."

Dayu

Half human, half Nighlok, Dayu has survived in the Netherworld only because Master Xandred likes her music. Her loyalties to Master Xandred are suspect, though, since she has a dark secret: she traded her human life centuries ago to a powerful Nighlok in order to save her one true love...Deker! The only possession she was allowed to take from the human world was her precious guitar. Although the guitar has now transformed into the grotesque 'Harmonium', Dayu still loves it above all else.

"Here's a tune with some edge!"

Moogers

Wicked creatures who squirm into our world through gaps in space and time, the Moogers exist only to serve Master Xandred. These foot soldiers aren't very smart and are usually easily defeated!

Nighloks

The Nighloks are creatures of the Netherworld who wreak havoc at Master Xandred's request. However, the time they can spend in our world is limited because they dry out and must return to the evil Sanzu River to replenish themselves! Here are some of the nastiest Nighloks...

ROFER

Rofer has very long arms that can punch through solid ground and concrete so he can attack his victims from underground. He'll serve you a knuckle sandwich!

DOUBLETONE

Doubletone is a sneaky monster who tricks victims into giving up their dreams.

DREADHEAD

An incredibly strong Nighlok, most of the Power Rangers' weapons don't work on him. Dreadhead is only defeated after the Red Ranger masters the powerful Beetle Disc.

YAMIROR

Yamiror is a monster with really stinky breath. The smell is so bad that it knocks the Rangers out of action!

MADIMOT

Madimot can control minds. The Blue Ranger falls briefly under his power until he is saved by the Red Ranger.

DESPERAINO

This monster can conjure storms with raindrops that bring despair to those whom they fall upon.

ROBTISH

Robtish was originally sent to get rid of the Red Ranger by Master Xandred, but was stopped by Deker.

VULPES

Vulpes is a master of spying with his inter-dimensional mirror and uses it to try to discover Jayden's secret Sealing Symbol!

STEELETO

A strong Nighlok with the ability to use the blades on his body to attack his victims.

ANTBERRY

A slimy character, he fights his enemies by soaking them with slippery goo. Slimed, the Rangers have a hard time keeping hold of their weapons – and Antberry himself!

SPLITFACE

A really scary Nighlok, Splitface steals the spirits of his victims.

ARACHNITOR

Arachnitor plots with Octoroo to steal Master Xandred away and take over his throne by trying to discover the Red Ranger's Sealing Symbol.

RHINOSNORUS

With his dream mist, Rhinosnorus can put his victims in a deep sleep and then enter their dreams. Once in this dream world, he can devour them!

SCORPIONIC

Summoned by Master Xandred to scare the humans, Scorpionic is the first Nighlok to almost defeat the Red Ranger in battle.

NEGATRON

Negatron can get into the minds of his victims and make insults that turn their emotional pain into physical pain. He says, "If the truth hurts, excellent!"

Create a Nighlok!

Master Xandred is always looking for new Nighloks to help him defeat the Power Rangers! What do you think the ultimate Nighlok would look like? A barrel-shaped red monster that steamrolls into the Rangers? Or a slimy, warty monster that can steal your voice and leave you croaking like a frog?

Use your imagination and come up with the next badder-than-bad monster!

My new Nighlok is called

_____

It wears

_____

Its special powers are

_____

Its weapons are

_____

Its catchphrase is

_____

It makes humans cry by

_____

Now draw your new nasty Nighlok and add a catchphrase in the box!

HUMANS ARE A WASTE OF GOOD SPACE!

Nighlok Talk

The Nighloks may be the most evil, disgusting creatures ever to come out of the Sanzu River, but they do have some funny one-liners! Have a laugh at some of the best ones.

That all you got?

I'm cold as an iceberg but sting like a bee, it's tough to stop what you can't see!

Your swords ain't got no mojo!

Humans are a waste of good space!

You got a bad case of fistaphobia!

I won't be through till I clobber you!

This blast will be your last!

Could You Beat a Nighlok?

Samurai Ranger, will victory be yours?
Find out in this amazing quiz!

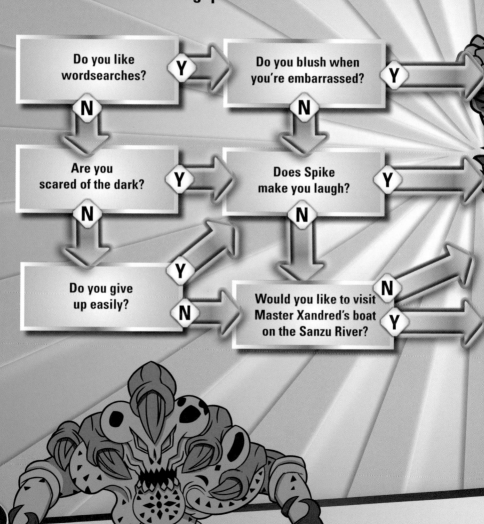

Do you like wordsearches?

Y → Do you blush when you're embarrassed?

N ↓

Are you scared of the dark?

Y → Does Spike make you laugh?

N ↓

Do you give up easily?

Y

N

Would you like to visit Master Xandred's boat on the Sanzu River?

N

Y

Would the Red Ranger be your best Ranger friend? **N**

Y

Would you shout "Take that, creep!" as you smashed a Nighlok? **N**

Y

Do you think you would be good with a sword? **N**

Y

NIGHLOK KNOCK!

You're not quite there, but with a little more practice, that Nighlok will be history!

NIGHLOK SHOCK!

He may be down, but he's not out! You gave him a big fright, but he's coming back for more.

GOODNIGHT, NIGHLOK!

Way to go! He won't be bothering anybody else!

Samurai Megazord!

We Are United.

When the Power Rangers need to defeat a MegaMonster Nighlok, they go into Mega Mode. The Zords they control grow extra large, and they can combine them to create super warrior robots!

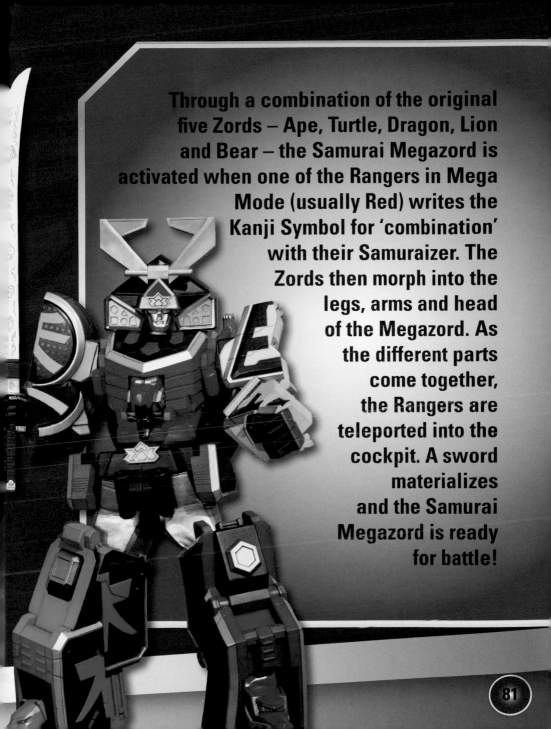

Through a combination of the original five Zords – Ape, Turtle, Dragon, Lion and Bear – the Samurai Megazord is activated when one of the Rangers in Mega Mode (usually Red) writes the Kanji Symbol for 'combination' with their Samuraizer. The Zords then morph into the legs, arms and head of the Megazord. As the different parts come together, the Rangers are teleported into the cockpit. A sword materializes and the Samurai Megazord is ready for battle!

Mega Megazords

Beetle Blaster Megazord

Created by combining the BeetleZord and the Samurai Megazord.

One of the secret Zords passed down from previous generations of Samurai, the BeetleZord represents the power of a regular Samurai Disc, making it twice as powerful!

The Red Ranger masters the Beetle Disc when confronted by Dreadhead. It allows him to upgrade the Fire Smasher to the mighty Five Disc Cannon. When Dreadhead transforms into a MegaMonster Nighlok, the Samurai Rangers form the Beetle Blaster Megazord to defeat Dreadhead for good!

Swordfish Fencer Megazord

Created by combining the SwordfishZord and the Samurai Megazord.

The SwordfishZord was lost long ago, but when it is spotted in the ocean, Jayden gives Kevin the mission of capturing it on his Catch Disc. After a long struggle, he finally reels in the Zord.

When the Samurai Rangers are confronted with stinky Yamiror, only the SwordfishZord can save them! When Kevin returns with the special Zord, it unleashes a healing rain and the Rangers regain their strength, forming the Swordfish Fencer Megazord to defeat the Nighlok!

Tiger Drill Megazord

Created by combining the TigerZord and the Samurai Megazord.

When the TigerZord is still under Madimot's control, he manages to cast a spell on Kevin, which forces him to attack his friends! Luckily, Jayden figures out how to break the spell and forms the Tiger Drill Megazord to destroy Madimot!

Samurai Battlewing

This aerial Megazord is formed when the TigerZord, the BeetleZord and the SwordfishZord combine. It is piloted by the Red, Green and Blue Rangers.

During a battle with Desperaino, the Red, Green and Blue Rangers summon their three new Zords and combine them into the Samurai Battlewing. With the help of the Samurai Megazord, the Battlewing defeats MegaMonster Desperaino!

Design a Megazord

What would you add to the Samurai Megazord to make it totally unbeatable? Would you use the Zord you made up earlier? Or would you want to try something new?

My Megazord is called

_____

_____

It's special because

_____

_____

Its weapons are

_____

_____

It defeats giant Nighloks by

_____

_____

Samurai Rangers, Zords combine!

Now draw a picture of your Nighlok-bashing Megazord below!

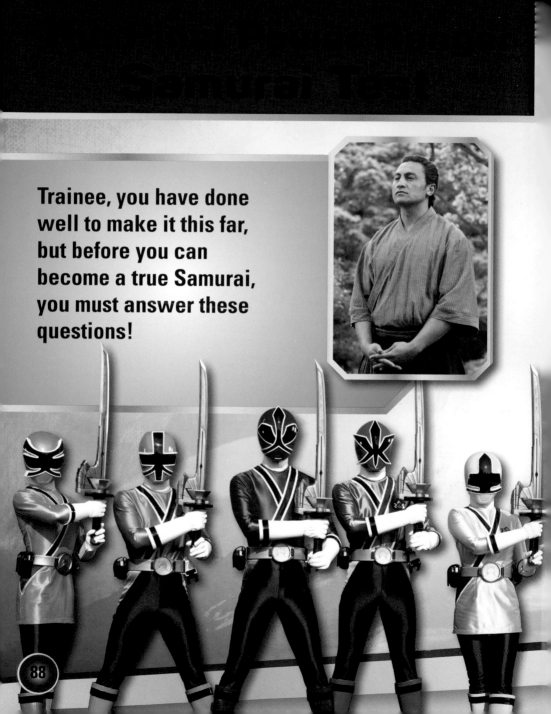

Trainee, you have done
well to make it this far,
but before you can
become a true Samurai,
you must answer these
questions!

1) What would you do if you came across Rofer, with two of the fiercest fists you've ever seen?

A Run away…screaming!
B Find a large rock and hide.
C Round up your fellow Rangers – the battle has just begun!

2) What would you do if a Nighlok called you a goody-two-shoes Power Ranger?

A Get upset and cry.
B Get angry and call him a noodle-faced loser!
C Don't let it get to you – he's just a mean-mouthed Nighlok.

3) What would you do if the Red Ranger kept beating you in sword training?

A Hide his sword so he can't practise as much!
B Go away in a sulk. Why is he so good?!
C Be supportive. He's supposed to be the best and you can learn from him.

4) What would you do if Master Xandred came to Earth and wanted to have a battle with you?

A Tell him you'll give him all the tears he needs for the Sanzu River!
B Tell him no, you're far too busy this week.
C Ask him "What's wrong with you? Didn't anyone ever hug you as a kid?!"

5) What would you do if one of your fellow Rangers was left behind in a battle?

A Get out of there – it's every Ranger for themself!
B Go back and check on them, but if they're winning, leave them to it.
C Get straight back. Rangers together, Samurai forever!

6) What would you do if you came across a Nighlok that you couldn't beat with your Spin Sword?

A Give up.
B Let him run away – it's not your problem.
C Try a Five Disc Beetle Cannon Fire Strike! That'll work!

7) What would you do if you tried Mia's cooking and it tasted terrible?

A Tell her "Yuck, that's gross!"
B Say that she might want to find a new hobby.
C Don't hurt her feelings and try to eat some of it!

8) What would you do if Emily was feeling homesick?

A Leave her to get on with it.
B Tell her to stop complaining because everyone feels that way sometimes.
C Talk to her about it, and then take her somewhere fun to help her feel better!

9) What would you do if you helped the Rangers defeat Master Xandred forever?

A Have a 'We beat the Nighloks' party!
B Go on holiday.
C Keep training – a Samurai Ranger should always be learning and improving.

Mostly As

Oh, dear. You have a little more work to do, trainee, but don't give up!

Mostly Bs

So close! The other Rangers have all been where you are. Keep practising!

Mostly Cs

You are Samurai Ranger ready! Turn over the page for your Trainee Certificate!

Rangers Together, Samurai Forever!

Ranger Trainee Certificate

You've made it, trainee!
Mentor Ji is very impressed with you.
Those nasty Nighloks will think twice
before messing with you.
Go, Go Samurai!

✂ Ask an adult to help you cut out your certificate.

_____

(Sign your Power Ranger name here!)